GROWING PAINS

Wisdom from a Teenaged Sage

JEWEL MASSIAH

GROWING PAINS
Wisdom from a Teenaged Sage

Copyright © 2020 by Jewel Massiah
This title is also available as a Kindle e-book.
Visit www.amazon.com

All rights reserved. This book or any portion thereof may not be copied or reproduced for commercial gain or profit. The use of short quotations or occasional page copying is permitted for book review or discussion purposes only, and with the written permission of the author or publisher.

Front Cover Artwork: Lisa-Marie Lord

Graphics: Stephan Massiah

Printed in the United States of America by:
Kindle Direct Publishing

First Printing: September 2020

ISBN-13: 978-976-95780-5-0

E-Book ISBN: 978-976-95780-6-7

Published by: OTBox
JOTBox Ltd.
66 Faralon Drive, Bel-Air,
La Romaine, Trinidad and Tobago
E-mail: jotboxltd@gmail.com

DEDICATION

To Stephan:

When I was younger, you walked into my room and said,

"Stop crying about it. Write about it."

I've never put the pen down since...

Contents

Falling

I listen to your snores

As if they were piano keys

With every breath you breathe,
There's a life that needs me

"I fell in love the way you fall asleep:
slowly, then all at once..." (The Fault in
Our Stars (2012), John Green. New York, Penguin
Books USA, 2012, eBook)

Slowly, yet clumsily

Harsh, but at peace

Your silent hums reassured your ease
But your desperate cries awakened
seas

With every breath you breathe,
There's a life that needs me

So breathe, so fall, so sleep

Because while I felt weak

And in search of safety

Here comes this life

That lays his head on me safely

Doesn't he know I'm not strong
enough to save the both of us?

But here's the funny thing

That your presence taught me about
myself

When there's a life depending on me,
I will always find strength.

Here's the hardest part of forming and forging any type of relationship that no one tells us about:

<u>**Vulnerability.**</u>

The strongest bonds I have ever made have been with those who let their walls fall in spite of all the risks that lay ahead of us.

My favourite thing about this poem is <u>someone actually needed me</u>.

Being needed validates you in some strange way, and it's funny, because people need people every single day. So why does it seem so strange and exclusive to be needed?

Pride.

I bet you're sitting holding this book, needing someone and denying it. Whether it be your parents, a friend, a sibling or even that dumb teenage boy, life is too short to save your ego and sacrifice relationships. So go ahead and love them openly and if your heart gets ripped out and stamped on, well I've got a chapter on that too.

Sadly this is the reality of life. Behind every giant risk is the greatest amount of happiness you'll ever find, and that type of happiness is 100% worth the heartache. Every. Single. Time.

In this life, let the walls down and be open. Never give anyone the benefit of making you love less. They don't deserve that type of power.

To the person who opened up and let their guard down so that I could be there for them, thank you. That night, I learnt a lot about myself, I can save someone even while I'm drowning; I can make you feel calm even when all I feel is anxiety; I can protect you even when I am being attacked.

People help us find the superhero within ourselves, the second someone we love cries out for help.

Guilt

*All I heard was the deafening sound
of silence*

*As the ringing in my ears echoed the
mistakes I made*

*Many say it happens, disappointment
fades*

*Life goes on, and yet I feel as though I
am an island*

*Alone, awaiting a sneak attack I know
I am unable to defend against*

Awaiting my death

*Fronting as if I am brave enough to
fight weapon-less*

*Blindfolded, like an unprepared
student who walks into a test*

Underneath it all I cry, tearless

But emotion-filled

*A warrior whose will to fight had
been killed*

*Then came the love of those around
me lifting me to my feet*

*Then came an embrace tenderly from
the monsters I thought I had to defeat*

*Love in the most unexpected places is
the definition of strength*

*What I thought were my trials were
the blessings you sent.*

'm going to tell you guys a true story, no details held back.

This poem was written the day I brought home my first and last letter of suspension from school.

Seven entire days! The maximum by the way. I drank alcohol in school, White Oak rum to be specific, and no I am not proud of that, but if I had the chance to erase the situation, I would not.

I expected my parents to kill me. I expected to be given a suitcase and be shipped away. But that didn't happen.

Here's the thing about guilt that no one tells us:

<u>Guilt is not dependant on punishment or a lecture, as long as you've got a conscience and a heartbeat you WILL feel it.</u>

So my parents never saw it coming from a 'good child' like me; and I regret to have to admit how much they contributed to my bad decision. I take responsibility for my actions however, the truth behind it all is I was tired of being the good child whose good behaviour was never appreciated. So one day I woke up and stopped caring about making anyone proud. I am a little ashamed of that phase, but in that moment, I honestly stopped caring.

My advice to any parent reading this page is simple...highlight the good things your children do. Often times, every mistake and error is blasted and never forgotten, but the many times we do our best are sorely overlooked.

I still felt sick; I still felt like the worst disappointment to ever walk the earth. That is when I learnt we don't change because our parents tell us to; we don't cry because they punish us. It is all something that comes from within us...when WE want to change, when WE see our wrong and when WE feel compelled to correct it.

If there are any parents reading, I really hope you would take note of this. If your child is ever gonna be the man/woman you one day hope for them to be, the key is to teach them right from wrong. There comes a point where you can no longer force them to make the right decision. You need to lay a strong foundation to prepare for that day; and yes, they will mess up and make mistakes but as long as they feel guilt, you have effectively taught them right from wrong, and you have done your job. Now give them space to grow.

I hope that when we feel guilty about our actions, we understand that we're not a bad person. Bad people never feel guilty and even if they do, they never change. The moment you feel the need to right your wrongs, you can assure yourself that you are a decent human being who made a mistake.

You will make more mistakes and that's okay. Your job is to make sure you never make the same one twice.

Karma

*I'm becoming every flaw I've pointed
out in others*

*My hypocritical screams stifle the
pain that I've tried to cover*

*Think twice before you stop to judge,
stop to point fingers*

*One day I woke up inflicting the same
pain that once lingered*

I'm anger in its purest form

I am hate as an element

*I'm the same monster that I once
scorned*

I am the karma that was never sent

I will scream it from the top of my lungs

Then whisper, "That's not what I said though"

I will wreak havoc and create storms

Then cry when there's no rainbow

Inflicting pain on others while others inflicted pain on me

If another made me flinch, I will make the others scream

I am a hurricane, I am dangerous, as unexpected as a tsunami

I intend to do damage, but I will swear I moved gently

I'm anger in its purest form

I am hate as an element

I'm the same monster I once scorned

I am the karma that was never sent

Do not glare at me like I'm evil, don't pretend to be scared

Because you're the closest thing I've met to the devil, and he laughs at the thought of fear.

I have had an ugly, angry phase. In as much as I would love to hate, in as much as I deserved to be furious, truth be told, I could never find it in my heart to hate people.

This poem was everything I felt but could never do. It's honestly big cap.

I remember I was supposed to be studying for a Chemistry exam when I sat by the dining table, writing this poem. Memorizing definitions I came across the word "element". It was that night I learnt an element is a substance which cannot be broken down into anything simpler; it is pure.

There came the whole idea of hate as an element, pure hatred, which cannot be broken down into anything else because it is simply hatred.

I want to burst the bubble of any "savage"/"cold-hearted" person reading this.

Here's the thing about hate that no one tells us:

<u>You cannot hate what you have never loved.</u>

Let me build on this peculiar truth...you cannot hate what you don't currently care about. Therefore I laugh at anyone who thinks that hating something makes you tough because it doesn't. It actually makes you hurt. And it's okay to admit that you're hurt rather than hiding behind your claims of feeling nothing at all. I am here to break the news to you that the person who comes to mind when you hear the word "hate" is someone you love a lot. Someone whose actions hold weight.

So choose wisely who you give that type of power to.

If you want my honest advice, I don't think you should hate anyone. If you no longer want anything to do with them just exit their lives. You can choose to cheer the loudest when they accomplish something, even when they'll never hear you. You can remove yourself from people's lives, from toxic situations and anything stifling your growth **_without_** allowing hate to be born.

Love unapologetically.

Love even when it hurts.

Love unconditionally.

Never give anyone the power to stop you from loving.

Untitled

5 months since we've spoken, since our hearts had been opened

To a chapter of a book I had not chosen

To read.

I held you as if no one else had ever held me

But if you hold something you don't know is broken whom do you blame when you bleed?

They told me a poem is a glance into the writer's heart that you see

If I am a poet and you are my poetry

Then my broken words reflect a broken you, create a broken me.

*I'd rather not say you made a broken
me, but more so you opened me*

*My eyes now trained to awe at your
beauty*

You are art

*The underrated kind found in the back
of a 9 year old Picasso's paper*

Doodled on the back of a book

Doodled on the back of my book

Carved into the cracks of my heart

*Though dark, you found your way
through*

So I refused to want to love you

*And boy were my instincts right but
my actions did not follow through*

I still fell hopelessly in love with you

Even though you are gone, I use the empty space of your ghost to fall deeper

The poet that poured her love into poetry that just refused to keep her.

Fever? The damage you did was much deeper

Cancer, you were a cancer

Sometimes a horoscope really is the answer, the warning, and disclaimer

Not to hurt your ego but our chemistry was the chemo

As I chose to cure the sickness I felt without you

Well I'd lose my dignity, my sanity falling too

As we grew in chemistry as chemo, unaware that the cancer was you

What do you do when the cure is the illness and the illness is the cure?

I chose to be sick, I wanted it

Endured so much only to see that you left regardless

So my dreams were farfetched

If only I had known that you were bleeding

Now that I see you are healing

Even with my eyes closed I still see it

Even without the cancer the chemo is still needed

Just let me love you past the hurricanes you've been enduring,

For once let me do the curing

Stop writing the story. I am the poet

*When you hold something you don't
know is broken, whom do you blame
when you bleed?*

I blame the thing that is broken

*For letting me hold it and cut myself
unknowingly*

*With pride too high to admit you
were struggling behind that screen*

So I blame you for the pain that I feel

You cut me deep, you let me bleed

*You allowed me to fall to my death,
into love and I can't get up*

*I wish you were still in my presence as
much as you are present in my
thoughts*

But you're not

*It's transparent and we see the
reality, you see the real in me*

I've opened gracefully

*Is there any hope for the broken you
to love a broken me?*

know this poem is extremely long.
Yes, this poem is as real as it gets.

No, I will not give you the tea on how
my heart was stomped on.

But here's the thing no one tells us
about love:

**Just because someone loves you
today doesn't mean they'll love you
tomorrow.**

**Someone who falls out of love is not a
monster, they are simply human.**

Funny enough though, the person this
poem is written about never loved
me, and yes it's ridiculous to sit

around and write a poem about heartbreak when someone never asked for your heart in the first place. He was never my boyfriend, never spoke about forever, never said he needed me to survive. But he said to me, "You are the most talented girl I've ever met."

No teenage boy ever sat down and listened to my covers or my clumsy fingers dance across piano keys with everything except grace. No boy had ever begged me to sing for him for days until I gave in, until him. I wasn't just a pretty girl to him, in fact, he called me beautiful. He called me intelligent and well...quite annoyed...he called me overly optimistic. So I chose to love him, which isn't fair to him because he never signed up for such strong emotions. And if he ever reads this book, lingering on this page, he probably won't even know I was writing about him. I know for a fact he never loved me; never promised me anything, yet I still felt as if my husband had died the day we stopped speaking.

It was from him I learnt the lesson of love never being an obligation, no matter how much you wish it was. It sounds horrid, but it's actually very beautiful. You look at those who choose to love you every day and find a new level of appreciation for them, because the reality is, they can stop loving you whenever they want and it's not a crime. It is actually one of the things that makes us human: **<u>free will.</u>**

So dear broken-hearted soul or heartbreaker reading this page, please remember to follow your heart wherever it leads you, and let people go wherever their heart leads them. Stop playing the blame game and no longer blame yourself.

I publicly challenge the saying "If you love someone let them go." I challenge it with my theory "If you don't love someone, set them free" and "If you love yourself, let go of anything that does not contribute to that love."

However if you do love someone then the saying is very simple, "Love them."

If they don't love you, they'll set you free and if you love yourself, my dear, you will allow them to do so.

Love sounds like a complicated tongue-twister but it really isn't.

Live

In this world of chaos

*To every action you put out, there's a
reaction that is sent*

*Don't be concerned with their
reaction, but be concerned with your
intent*

*Just smile and live your life with no
apologies at all*

*The day you look for their acceptance,
is the same day that you'll fall*

I wasted a long period of my life trying to fit in. High school is one of the scariest pressure-filled environments. It is very easy to lose yourself trying your hardest to keep up with every new trend, while you don't even notice the subtle ways in which your true identity fades. I don't know if I am the only one who has felt this or maybe I am the only person willing to admit it.

There were times when it mattered more to me how people viewed something rather than what the reality was.

Nobody has life figured out in their first year of high school, sometimes not till the end of it all. Some people can never truly find the courage to unapologetically be themselves, while everyone else who does, has a very different way of doing it. This world is truly chaos, and you will never find peace in trying to be a part of it. Everyone is going to react to who you decide to be.

Maybe you'll end up like me and wake up one morning with a Facebook post trending about you, with all the most popular people in school liking and sharing, with people who you thought were your friends commenting, then enduring the hushed whispers as you get to school the next day. Maybe that's what it took for me to finally search for myself again. In that moment, I realized these people I wanted to be like had absolutely no conscience or heart. So, I stayed up the entire night crying, feeling absolutely worthless, and I hope that was worth all your laughter.

I am truly grateful for every single one of you especially the boy who created the post. Thank you for waking me up! Imagine I almost became one of you when I had the opportunity to be this beautiful human I am today.

I learnt the rule of life: make sure your heart is in the right place with every action you put out into the universe, and as long as it is, DO WHATEVER YOU WANT SIS. This is your story, you are the author. **Critics don't get paid more than the author.**

This page was hard to type. This page is raw. I am openly discussing one of my lowest points in life. I need to warn you how ugly it gets when you care about people's approval but let you know how awesome life is when you never look back to hear their reactions. Be yourself and let them talk.

You have two options.

You can be the person who talks about people's lives or you can be the person who has a life worth talking about.

You can become what they want you to be or you can be something that they strive to become.

You can be popular or you can simply **be.**

Right now, my bullies are reading my book. They just put food on my table.

Honestly, people's opinions hurt. To this day, I still find myself feeling embarrassed about that Facebook post even though I have regained my power and self-worth as an individual. It honestly still stings; it still makes me cry; it still makes me think twice before I enter a room.

My point is it's no bed of roses and if you're reading this chapter you already know that. It's a choice you have to get out of bed every morning and one I make. So, despite the fact that I'm still scared they'll laugh at me, I'm still going to be myself.

Life gets better.

Even though the memories still haunt me, I still choose to see myself as stronger after experiencing what I did.

Even though it still stings, I am grateful for those people who pushed me to truly search deep enough to find myself.

Hopefully one day it won't hurt anymore but for now, I refuse to let the pain stop me.

Tornado

*My lover walked into my life like a
tornado*

*Every ounce of stability my life once
had, crashed*

*And each storm I avoided to paint my
fake rainbows*

*In one split second came tumbling
back*

*You were the sunshine that brought
rain*

The Joy that brought pain

*This bittersweet love sends me mad
till I'm drained*

*This bittersweet love is what's
keeping me sane*

You touched scars under scabs that
I've spent years hiding

The ears that heard me scream were
the same ones I'd confide in

He is a force to be reckoned with, my
lover's a storm

He is my chaos, he is cold but he
keeps me warm

Some nights I hate you for making me
face these demons

But since you came I've never fought
alone, you're the shoulder I lean on

Most nights I love you for giving me
safety

But the moment you leave, life grabs
my neck and shakes me

And somewhere out there while
you're peacefully sleeping

I'm trying my best to stop these wounds from bleeding

My lover's a storm but here's the beauty in that

He scared the crap out of my demons and they're afraid to fight back

My greatest love story of all time is actually the "ugliest". This was the first interaction I ever had with someone who forced me to show parts of myself I hadn't learned to accept yet. I had to dig in to the scars of my past. You see I was once that person who gave everyone the version of myself I wanted them to see. My teachers saw the scholar, my friends saw my wisdom, my family saw my bravery, but this boy stuck around long enough to meet the broken me.

It's what made this kind of love a challenge.

I was afraid to open up, afraid to get attached, afraid to be vulnerable, but most of all, I was ashamed of my past.

To this day, I still cringe when revisiting some of these memories. Don't we all wish that people could fall in love with a perfect version of us?

Well, we honestly shouldn't because it is so much more beautiful for people to fall in love with our ugliest parts, and still find perfection in the midst of our broken pieces.

Here's the thing no one tells us about real love: **It is the most catastrophic storm that will ever hit your life.**

When you're used to toxic people and one-sided relationships, your very first breath of genuine sacrificial love will stifle you.

My life had turned upside down. I was digging in to parts of myself I had purposefully buried out of necessity because this love was no longer surface level.

One of the most important things I will ever tell you is: if you run away from the scary parts of your life, if you cover up all the experiences and put a nice pretty bow on top, you will only ever be able to love yourself on the surface.

The deepest relationship you should ever have with a human being should be with yourself. When "Mr. Right" shows up, best believe he's coming with his shovel to go to the lowest points of your life and he'll be taking notes.

This process will make you uncomfortable; it will allow the voices in your head to get louder; your insecurities will sky rocket, then your perfect life will crumble.

This rule applies to friendships, family and romantic relationships. As long as a deep connection is being formed, the storm will begin. A truly beautiful thing because your demons don't like it when you look them in their eyes. They have no control when you finally decide to shed light on your story. Facing the ugly truth and traumatic experiences help the healing process; help you to connect to other humans without your baggage sneaking up on you, ultimately helping them to know exactly how you need to be loved.

When preparing for a disaster there are a list of precautionary measures to take.

When facing any relationship storm the instructions are simple: Embrace it.

Cheers

Cheers to your existence, to the involuntary muscles that make your heart beat,

Their persistence.

For loving closely while the world around you seems distant

Your visions, of connecting to something.

A heart that begs to feel and scars that pretend to heal.

Cheers because you're still here

This shot is for your fears, ones like getting out of bed in the morning

Cheers because you exist in the midst of them.

*Take for granted that our panting
means we'll breathe forever*

*As if we're not gasping for air, as if
we're not running a race,*

*Faster than the tears run down our
face.*

*They pretend we are always happy,
insomnia is trendy*

*Because at 3:00 a.m no one's really
sleeping*

*Our tired eyes bother no one as long
as we're still seeing*

*No one's gonna ask what that sad
quote meant until you kill yourself*

*The girl who cuts is only an attention
seeker until she's dead, no one hears
the quiet girl until she's gone*

Then they'll quote every word she said.

But cheers to you, she hasn't shed more tears than you do

The difference is, you're still here

Some days you find it in yourself to smile larger than space

But on your bravest days you put a smile on someone else's face.

Through your puffy eyes you've seen people's beauty, comforted others selflessly

You deserve to exist forever, because sadness will never defeat you

Cheers to your happiness

*That you've formed in the same way
God formed Adam when he created
the earth*

Out of dirt

You've created happiness out of dirt

*Thank you, for pretending to know
your worth*

Until it became reality.

I don't care what anyone else says, we deserve gold medals for staying alive!

I feel like no one gives you enough credit for the amount of strength it takes for you to drag yourself out of bed every day.

Here's the thing no one tells us about existing: **Thank You.**

There are hidden voices in everyone's mind, which make us feel as though we are not equipped with what it takes to accomplish all the things we aim for every day. There are moments when we feel weak, moments where we feel ugly, moments where we feel like failures and moments where we feel like all of our efforts go unappreciated. I want to be that random person in your life who finally makes you feel heard.

What makes life easier? Perspective.

Circumstances could always be devastating; you will always be stuck with the skin you're in, the household you were born into and know that toxic people will always try their best to disturb your peace. The only thing we actually have control over is our mind-set. So live in moments that make you laugh until your stomach burns. Stop being that person who misses all the fun because they're always stuck in their head overthinking what they have to go home to. Pretend that the good moments are going to last forever *even when* you know they won't. Put your happiness first and enjoy the breaths of fresh air because who knows when you'll get to feel this ecstasy again!

The world is honestly what you make it. Forget reality and write your own story. In **my** reality right now, I'm a best-selling author with hundreds of books sold, though in actuality I'm just a teenager typing her heart out on her mother's laptop. But the perspective I choose to accept will determine the way my entire life plays out.

So, I choose to see myself as the best until it actually happens one day. I like to pretend that every time I'm around people I love, we're going to be there forever and never have to leave. I know there's this philosophy that in order to truly appreciate moments we must spend each one as though it were our last, but I challenge this theory with one of my own, "Treat the amazing moments as if they were eternity, as if you held infinity in the palms of your hands."

As for the things in life that cause pain, remember that they are just the 5 second advertisement in the middle of your favourite movie. So instead of dwelling on them, remember to click that "skip" button and go back to being the absolute best version of yourself.

Instead of telling myself "You only live once," I've learnt to tell myself "You only live forever."

And this statement is 100% factual because your forever ends with you. You won't miss a single day of your eternity so relax and remember to exist.

Growing Fever

*So if it's too hard to speak, let your
tears draw the words unto your face
and I will read it.*

*You hunger for peace and beg for
healing*

*You think that I don't see it, the subtle
trickles of your heart bleeding*

*There's way more to your story than
the dark chapters you see*

*Grow into everything I have called you
to be*

*I'm going to let giants fight you and
mountains stand in your way*

*I'm going to let you feel these growing
pains.*

This is half of a poem I once wrote.

I was really struggling with becoming the young woman I am today with all this responsibility and pressure placed on me.

The first thing I did was pray about it because I thought God was getting a good laugh out of watching me suffer, but His response to me was utterly humbling. I think as we get older, we overcomplicate the simplest of things. We are not required to have all the answers to life; to have every aspect figured out. One day at a time, one stage a time, one battle at a time, and most importantly, one prayer at a time. It doesn't matter what your religion is, whenever life gets overwhelming remember that God has all the answers and thankfully, He loves you more than anything else in the universe. It's like taking a difficult class but also being the teacher's favourite. All you've got to do is ask for help.

Here's the thing about growing up no one tells us:

<u>The older you get, the harder life becomes.</u>

I know that growing up all we ever wanted to be were teenagers and as teenagers, all we want to be are adults. But the truth is, with age comes responsibility and expectations and as beautiful as life itself is, it's also a very serious task to stay alive. Take life one day at a time and when it gets too hard, take it one hour at time and when that gets too hard, take it one minute at a time. And if even that becomes too hard, take it one breath at a time. Yes. Breathe. Every breath is an accomplishment.

Growing pains are a beautiful reminder you're growing.

A reminder that you are stronger. A reminder that you are one step closer to your destination. So enjoy the journey.

PERSONAL UPDATE: I am adding this an entire year after I began, having felt way more intense growing pains...in fact right now, I find the pain to be unbearable!!! And the only thing keeping me going is my writing, more specifically, this book. I have this little hope that someday my words will be valued and touch hearts; someday God will use this gift He has placed in me. On that day, all this heartache will seem like preparation which helped me to get there. One day, these tears will be the very water my purpose used to grow. This is what keeps me going.

My Brother

*Our brother who art in heaven, and
our Father who protects him*

Can you even hear me?

*I wish there was a way to look into
your eyes, to argue one more time.*

*Anything other than holding you in a
wooden box, anything other than
stillness where you once could never
sit still.*

*The truth is every day I wait for you to
appear*

Please be somewhere

*In this room laughing at me, please
grant me peace*

*And Chris, my brown boy, if you're
really gone*

*Give us your loved ones the strength
to move on.*

*Move on to levels of life you never got
the chance to*

*Let us be the greatness we once saw
in you*

*I pray for your mother's heart, may it
be filled with whatever made you
prance around the world like you
owned it*

*I pray for the ones most broken but
try not to show it*

*I pray for every life you have
impacted without even knowing*

*Family, friends, classmates, co-
workers, strangers and me*

*I won't listen to the voices that tell
me to give up, the ones that say I'm
not strong enough*

I'd rather hear the voices of my brother who art in heaven and our Father who protects him.

Though your image of stillness has left us in shock, we know you're dancing beyond that wooden box.

My first experience with death.

The first time I'd seen someone every single day, then never saw them again.

It honestly makes me want to scream sometimes. It hurts so much!

Here's the thing no one tells us about death:

<u>There is no such thing as "moving on."</u>

You never move on, but you're forced to move forward.

My first death. It is still fresh. As I pen these words, two days prior was the 6 month anniversary. His name **is** Chris, well at least that's what we called him, and behind his back I'd call him "Indian Bird." The reason behind that name is an entirely different story on its own. It's hard to write about this because I feel like my family really believes I need to stop crying about it, but for so many reasons I cannot. His life was taken and nobody wants to explain to his loved ones what really happened that night.

I remember being told he was in the hospital. I read the message, brushed it off and went to sleep. Upon falling asleep, I dreamt that I went to visit him and he was okay...everything was okay. Then I jumped out of bed panic-stricken, opened my phone, read the message again and then it registered...my friend is in the hospital. I started to mentally plan to go visit him and eventually fell asleep again.

When I woke up, I put my clothes on for church but purposefully wore something casual so that I could pass by the hospital afterward. As I was walking out my front door, I saw the message from his brother indicating his death. I looked at those words and stopped moving. I broke down and couldn't get the pain to stop.

I wish I could go back to those moments of hope, the moments where I thought I'd see him again and he'd recover. The moments where I was certain all it would take was a few hospital visits...but in reality...it took none. Unfortunately, it all moved too fast. I had to work at a show the next day plus exams began that week. Life did not give me any time to process it.

As things progressed, I had to become the strong friend for everyone around me. I held everyone up in the wakes. I held their hands in the funeral. I even sat on the floor with them until they had the strength to get up and feel okay. Then, I helped my other friends make it through exams. I checked on his family as much as I could. I did my best and barely broke down.

Yet guys, there is this hollow feeling in my stomach whenever I think about him.

Death is the greatest growing pain of them all.

Chris has taught me so much though unfortunately, I only began to learn the lessons in his absence. Chris, I am sorry. I am so sorry for all the ways in which I failed you.

My advice is to learn from people while they are here. Experience them. Tell them you love them. If you fight, ask yourself if this fight is big enough to stop you from attending their funeral. If it's not, then humble yourself and fix it.

To those who have lost someone, I am here to take the pressure to "move on" off of you. Take your time baby, cry as many times as you need to, talk about them as much as you want to. Just remember that you have no choice but to move forward because everything that person believed you would accomplish and be, they're waiting in heaven to see it fulfilled.

Love is the greatest motivation of all. This one is for you Brownboy; I love you.

Summertime Fling

I fell in love with my summer-fling

Found myself giving this person everything

Knowing that when the summer sun sets and the leaves fall

I'll forget how to find the time to check on them

When it's September I'll forget to remember to ask if you've eaten

When it's Fall I'll forget to call and ask how you're sleeping

In October, you and I, we'll barely be speaking

And I'll lose track of the months as the cycle keeps repeating

My self-love is a summertime fling

Cause I don't have the discipline

I keep forgetting how to love myself, I can't do it everyday

When the summer sun sets and the sky gets darker, my self-worth slips away

I am terrible at consistency, especially when it comes to being consistent with myself.

I don't eat properly (or at all), I don't sleep enough, and I don't give myself the kindness I deserve. Sometimes, I make these huge plans to do better and they always fall through. I realized that I am in a toxic relationship with myself and have absolutely no idea how to break up with her.

She promises me she'll call me beautiful more often, then spends hours critiquing every single picture I post. She sends me to rehearsals on an empty stomach and believes that is "prioritizing". Mind you, she is never satisfied with the work I put in.

I hesitated to write about this as I haven't quite figured out how to love myself properly as yet. And this truth made me feel unqualified to give any advice.

However, my recent decision is even though I may not have yet mastered "it", I'll still share my journey, what I've learnt and am learning along the way.

Here's the thing no one tells you about self-love: **You can't live without it but you'll die "trying" to find it.**

The thing is, we are ever-changing beings. As soon as you fully understand and accept this version of yourself, a new one is born tomorrow. There is no "the end" in this love story but we still can't afford to close the book.

We will spend forever reading, trying, failing, succeeding, giving up and starting over. Even the most stable person in the universe has to work on their self-love every single day. So, make it your duty to get to know yourself every day because you can never love what you don't fully understand. You can try, but you will fail to love that person or thing in the way it deserves to be loved.

I remember after my first experience with death, I completely changed and did not understand it all. Interested in things I used to hate, detached from people I once couldn't live without and longing for things I thought I'd never need.

Jewel needed a new type of love from herself, and if I didn't crack that code, I'd still be waking up feeling unfulfilled and alone.

Today, you might be doing yourself a favour by putting pressure on yourself to be productive. But tomorrow, you might need someone to tell you it's okay if you rest. Your needs are always evolving.

Self-love is more than just being comfortable in the skin you're in, it's also learning about that skin every day. It's giving that skin the nutrients it needs to grow and knowing when its diet has changed.

I love myself and every day I fall in love with her all over again.

This is one chapter we will never have completely figured out. This is a process where you will always be "trying" and somehow that means you've already succeeded.

The Potter's Touch

*His hands slammed violently as it
collided with her body*

*But clay does not make much more
than a muffled sound*

*She is silenced and shaped, with
perfect purple plastered on her face*

DADDY ISSUES 101

It took me some time to realize that this is my story and I have the right to be my own narrator. So, if it offends you that I have found the strength to speak about this, I am very sorry but I need to.

Let me start by saying that I love my father and he has helped me become the amazing young lady I am today, and for that I owe him utmost respect.

The relationship we have presently is a vast improvement from what it once was. I thank God for that.

The truth of the matter however, is he was the first male to ever break my heart. The problem is, he wanted perfection and perfection is impossible. The bible says spare the rod and spoil the child. The bible should've also mentioned if you swing the rod too hard you'll kill the child.

Discipline can very easily become abuse. As a parent, you really need to evaluate whether "Am I hitting my child because I want them to know right from wrong, *or* am I hitting them simply because I am angry, disappointed and have no clue what to do with these emotions?"

I was never a bad child. Even if I was, I never deserved the things I encountered, and did not even recognize what was transpiring until many years down the line. So many days, I wished to disappear, feeling as though I couldn't breathe for years, feeling unloved and scared all the time. To this day, I still think he'd say "When you're older and mature you'll look back and appreciate this." **NO!** I will never appreciate the bruises or the headaches or the way your eyes would look dead and angry. If only you could see yourself.

I used to adore you. Every day waiting by the door for you to come home just to be the first person to tell you hello. All you ever needed to do was ask me to work on something or explain what you wanted me to do. I was always seeking your approval, and would've changed in a heartbeat for you. Even if I failed, I'd try harder the next time.

But such adoration has now morphed into fear; I am afraid of you. Yes I have become the very well behaved individual perhaps you envisioned, but random panic attacks now plague my soul, sweet sleep null and void for half my life, anxiety my bittersweet companion simply to come home. Every time you pass by me, I flinch. Does it make you feel proud? Is this who you wanted me to become? Are you even sorry? Do you know I am going to have to live with this for the rest of my life? Is this what love is? Is this what I should search for in a man?

Let me know.

Without you ever fully understanding the situation, I have still managed to forgive you. Undoubtedly, I see that you have become an entirely new person, and I am so very proud of you. Your self-development does not go unnoticed. It must've been a lonely road sometimes. I want you to know that you will never be alone again. We are your backbone, your support system and we love you.

Here's the thing no one tells you about generational curses:

<u>You cannot beat something you're afraid to face.</u> For this reason alone, I'm not going to avoid this situation. You can go your entire life successfully avoiding something and the next time you encounter it, is in the mirror.

I will be better. I know better and will do better.

I know you had intentions to do better but missed the mark because you never faced it. I am facing you, with open arms. I understand your perspective and see many things about you that I would like to be, but I also see the things in which I wish to be better.

Pray for the people who have caused you pain; understand that it is just a percentage of the pain they feel inside. Do not allow them to hurt you. Draw the line and stand up for your mental and physical health.

Call them out on their actions, hold them accountable, let the process of love be your guide. Listen to their side and choose to heal together.

BUT!

If your life is in danger, run for your life! Get very far away, to a safe space and place.

Love

*The most dangerous thing passed
between soul-mates*

Is in fact, love

*The thing that makes you leap miles
even when you're afraid*

*Attempt to fix, even when you're
broken*

*Showcase parts of yourself you swore
you'd never open*

Love is so whack.

Love is very powerful. It is not something to be played with or taken lightly. Love is much more than butterflies in your stomach or sex. Love is a verb; love is a choice.

It is something shown in the midst of all other emotions, in the midst of all other circumstances. Someone who "loves" you when they're happy or horny but not when they're tired or stressed...that person doesn't love you. Too many times in my generation, I see people pouring out love to individuals who do not deserve them. I am a strong believer in loving everyone, but I draw the line when it comes to romantic love.

Not everyone deserves that particular part of your heart. These young men don't even put in 1/3 of the effort these queens deserve and yet, there she is crying on her bed and sulking through school the next day.

What should you look for when auditioning someone to give your heart to? Agape. The way God loves us, that's agape.

Why you may ask? Well that's the love your soul was created to depend on; it's the love that tests the human ability to put someone before themselves.

The thing is if you've never encountered the way God loves you then you will never know what standard to hold these 'waste-men' at.

Do you even fully understand how valuable you are? The kind of work someone needs to put in just to taste your lips? The kind of effort you need to see before they get the privilege of holding your hand?

Now this one is for my boys. You don't have to throw yourself at every girl with a pretty face. Stop falling in love with people who don't even have the depth for you to fall into.

These mistakes are only being made because we haven't taken the time to understand what love should look like. We haven't taken the time to truly understand how amazing we are. We haven't taken the time to realize that if someone walks out of our life, it's their loss.

I know we don't understand because that person left and you're still crying, or you still let them back into your life, or you're still praying for a future with them. I need you to dust yourself off and realize that you are art in a colour-blind world and poetry in an illiterate society. They can't see your value because it's a value they lack. So teach them how you should be handled.

In order to teach, you must first learn "What am I worth?" The answer to this question is written all over the bible and if you're not a Christian perhaps it's written in your holy book, whatever it may be called. In a nutshell, spend time with God and let Him show you what love is.

Here's the thing no one tells us about soul-mates:

<u>**You can't find a soul-mate till you understand your soul.**</u>

Do you know how beautiful it is to meet someone who sees your worth and shows it in their actions? Nothing can stand in between two people who hold each other at the highest possible standard. Two people willing to grow for and with each other.

It is amazing the things we would do for love. Fights can never last too long because you're always wondering if they're okay. Pride has no say because you cannot afford to lose them. Unconditional becomes a word you can feel and touch.

If you're stubborn like me, you'll take a while to learn how to express all these feelings. But in a healthy space there is absolutely no rush. You're learning together.

A family should be raised in nothing less than a household where mommy and daddy love each other the way God taught them to love.

If you fail to respect this rule you are selfish. Here come the household issues; the divorces, the domestic violence, the emotional abuse or even just the simple lack of appreciation. Do it the right way or don't do it at all.

My Mother's Love

She is a sunset, the kind that makes city buildings shine

She is the breath-taking blend of colours

Resting on the skyline

The thing the world revolves around

Reminds us of day and comforts us at night.

In my darkest moments, she is my natural source of light.

She is a sunset. She does her job even when it is time to rest.

Because she believes that light and warmth are things we all deserve to get.

*So even when the nighttime creeps,
she strains herself and fights the
moon.*

*That we may never encounter
darkness. The sun will never set too
soon.*

*I am in love with your colours, your
strength and all your stripes of love.*

*Your light is true and selfless, you give
and give til you have none.*

I wrote this for Mother's Day 2020.

My mother is an absolutely amazing woman and for many years, I failed to see the many ways in which she held our family together.

I want to apologize for all the times I've been a regular teenager, giving her attitude she didn't deserve. As I matured, I understood that my mother did the absolute best she could. My mother goes above and beyond every single day.

When everyone else gives up on you, a mother's love never will. She has never given up on me.

I plan to give my mother everything she ever dreamed of some day because she works tirelessly to make sure I lack nothing. Yes, she annoys me so much sometimes and yes, there are flaws I have noticed, but at the end of the day this woman carried me for 9 months then carried my fragile heart for 16 years and counting.

A relationship with your mother is honestly essential.

To those who were never given the opportunity to have this bond with their mothers, to those who have lost their mothers along their journey, to those motherly hearts that haven't been afforded the opportunity to have children of their own, this chapter is for you.

This is a chapter of life we cannot afford to move forward without. So look around you and find those who need motherly love in their life and provide it if you can.

If you lack this element then seek it; do not neglect your need for a nurturer. And do not assume this lack makes you inferior or needy.

Look around you and find a strong, loving woman who possesses the qualities and lifestyle you wish to have. A mother is much more than 9 months of pregnancy and hours of painful labour. A mother is much more than sharing the same DNA as someone.

A mother is patience that only God Himself can match, wisdom that only understanding can bring and empathy far beyond what the average heart contains.

If you're failing your children please take a moment to work on yourself and be the woman they need you to be. If your mother failed you please become everything she neglected to be.

I hope my words can create change and influence us to do better.

I want to live in a world where every heart receives the love it requires to flourish. For too many generations we've been walking around feeling empty...emptying others and creating vicious cycles.

Here's the thing no one tells us about Mothers:

<u>They aren't the star player, they aren't the coach, they're the humble water-boys.</u>

What does that mean? Well, they're the most underrated yet key component. If life were a football game then as a child I'd be the footballer, constantly learning the game and growing. A father would naturally begin to coach, giving me the tough love I need to be the best. In the heat of the game all I ever think about is the cheering from the stands and the things the coach has taught me.

The moment I mess up and drop down because I'm tired, the crowd gets disappointed and coach gets angry, but a water-boy picks me up and refreshes me so I can get back out there.

Behind the scenes my mother prays and provides. She is the water-boy of my life and she never sees my falls as failures, she sees them as the moments I need her most.

When you get back on the field and win the game, please remember there was someone in the background equipping you with everything you needed to keep going.

Thank you Ma.

Sexual Assault

I've locked doors and left them behind

Running from pain and getting lost in the moon

I've escaped to beautiful places with endless sunshine

But I didn't know that part of me was locked in that room

So what's the point of chasing rainbows?

If when you get there you're out of breath

Why run as far as the wind blows?

If your thoughts are your enemy you can't escape the threat

*The truth is, you'll never forget ...
every breath you take is a breath of
regret*

*One day, during your perfect new life
you'll feel empty*

*Your small frame thinks twice before
getting out of bed*

*Wonder how you feel hollow when
your blessings are plenty*

*How to revive the parts of you that
are dead*

*Is it worth it to leave the broken girl
behind?*

*Won't you miss the hope that
sparkled in her eyes?*

*Won't you feel guilty knowing all the
nights she's cried?*

*She prayed for you to get this far and
she's still not by your side*

You won't feel beautiful until you've learnt to love her scars

Count the marks on her body, see them glow like shooting stars

So you're successful but she's still locked in those rooms.

Have you really gotten far?

How can you be great if you still can't be who you are?

Yeah, it just got dark in here.

I'm afraid for the entire world to look at me like a victim…please don't. Please see my strength and find your strength in my story.

When I was 6 years old, I had been forced to do a lot of things I didn't understand or feel good about. Not by family members, thankfully, but by "friends". I don't know why, but I was born with this need to be accepted. I was told if I did what was asked...I'd be accepted. I wouldn't be alone anymore.

You might read this and think I was so dumb, but do you know what it's like to be invisible? Everyone around you is at war with each other, and you fade away somewhere in the background of your own life.

At home, it was all about my older siblings; my teenage sister having a secret boyfriend (as all teenagers do) and my older brother defying all forms of "the system" (which is code for he hated school and rules he didn't understand). My family had their hands full, and no one noticed that I was at war with my own body.

Every day, I knew what I was going to school to face, then come home wondering how to face God and how to face my family. It didn't matter though; they never saw me. And I guess that hurt more than any judgement ever could.

Somehow, I knew it was all my fault. Somehow, I was sure that I asked for it or at the very least allowed it. The details are very foggy because sometimes when something is very painful your mind protects you from it.

Yet, I still remember how it felt, how it feels and what it will always feel like to let your body be someone else's...begging to get it back.

I dialled my parents' numbers so many times when I came home from school, ready to finally speak up, but then I'd hang up.

That's the second time I ever felt a broken heart.

School was a war-zone, somewhere I had to keep quiet or they'd "tell everyone what I did".

So after at least a year, they found something else to do with their time. They left me alone. And funny enough none of them passed their exams to advance to the next class. So I was truly left all alone.

What does this have to do with this poem?

Well during 2018-2020, I realized that there were parts of myself I left behind because I was ashamed.

I'm accomplishing all these big things. Started my own business - Beyond the Box - and produced 2 successful events, plus I wrote a book.

I tell you, no one wanted these wins as much as the little girl crying her eyes out. She deserves to win with me, but I am so afraid to face her. I'm sorry I put her in those positions to be scared, and I'm sorry I couldn't stand up for her.

I won't let trauma run my life. This body is beautiful, perfect and MINE. I'm taking it back because I have that power. I also have the power to let others experience it, but for now, I think no one deserves this body as much as Jewel does. For years, I hadn't even seen it in the mirror but now, I can't go straight pass a reflective surface.

Here's the thing no one tells us about our body:

You see that blank space? Exactly. No one ever shuts their mouth when it comes to our bodies. To anyone reading this, please take your power back and empower the version of yourself that is most weak. Don't bury the painful memories, let them motivate you. I could've run away from home. I could've killed myself. I could've given up. But what did I do with my pain? I wrote a book; this book I am sharing with you.

I'll say it again. I wrote a book. Now what will you do with your story?

Stephanie

When the darkness gets too scary

Please hold me like we're little kids

*I'm the first one in the crowd
screaming for your little wins*

*You're the only one **this** proud to see
my little wings*

To watch me grow, fly.

*I'm the only one who believes you can
really touch the sky*

*I'm this close to telling our father I
should walk you down the aisle*

*Because we have walked everywhere
else together*

*Tell your husband he's lucky to sleep
next to gold*

To listen to your tears, they're your stories untold

You never talk about your day, so when you do

It's something he should listen to

You're something he should listen to

If he ever takes you for granted I'll be waiting to fill his shoes

Because I could spend forever loving you

I could be broken-hearted or depressed but I could never be alone

We could live on streets or get lost but we will always find home

In each other

My sister is my entire heart. She's growing up so fast, and I'll admit it is a little scary letting go, but I know that I have to. My entire life, I've shared a bed with this girl, and we've shared a couple secrets.

One of the scariest things in life is being alone. And yes, there were a lot of moments in my life where I felt alone, but the moments she held me through, outweigh them. Putting her in my book is probably a selfish move because I have no clue what lesson I can teach you through our relationship.

All I know is that I want everyone to have someone who makes them feel safe. Everyone should have a "sister" or even a "brother". We should strive to be that for someone. Many times without her ever knowing, she has kept me alive. It is beautiful to have someone to be excited with and to laugh at. Someone who didn't even know you were having a bad day, but they still made it better. I have a couple people in my life who are this level of amazing. Stephanie was my first.

She has hurt me before and I'm pretty sure I've done the same, so we're even. But what I have learnt in my few years on this earth is that life is too short to hold grudges over someone's imperfections. I always say, every time you fight with someone ask yourself "If they died today would I attend their funeral?" If you'd cry when they pass away, then please hold them while they're here.

Please cherish the people who check on you and come through when you need them.

Exercise your forgiveness because people deserve it.

Maybe some people are like me, so hurt that you believe no one is there for you and hell-bent on the idea of "I don't need anyone."

I've heard so many people say "I born [sic] by myself." Explain to me then, if your mother didn't push and your doctor didn't show up, where would you be? There are hidden angels in your life whom you probably haven't noticed because you're so focused on the people who are failing you.

That was my problem. I spent too much time remembering everyone who gave up on me, left me or did me wrong. I almost missed the opportunity to experience the beautiful people God placed in my life.

We wouldn't be alive if at least one person hadn't shown us kindness. Do you know who those persons are in your life? If you can't name them then I need you to dig deeper. Under all the hurt, that's where your gratitude is hiding.

Here's the thing no one tells us about family:

<u>They come in unexpected forms.</u>

<u>They are safe spaces.</u>

<u>They are anybody and everybody who feels like home.</u>

For a little while, my sister was the only thing that felt like family. I knew without a doubt that someone was fighting for me even when I didn't believe I was anything worth fighting for.

Our little family will always mean the world to me and my family has grown so much since then.

I've learnt to love everyone in this house with every ounce of my heart. I've gained friends I have been through everything with. I have my tiny little support system which keeps me going. They give me something to work for.

Dear A3LKSJ, thank you for giving me a family.

Dear everyone in my life, I honestly thank you so much for your little acts of kindness that keep me going every day.

In life people's characters are tested by how they treat you when you have nothing. But your character is proven by how well you treat people when you have everything.

Don't forget to be thankful.

About The Author

Jewel Massiah was born in Guyana, South America and migrated to Trinidad with her parents in December 2006.

Always an ambitious and focused individual, she knew quite early what her life's path would be.

Jewel possesses an exceptional aptitude for the arts, and devoted much of her time to music, drama, dance and poetry, eventually emerging as a prolific, self-taught spoken word artist.

In 2019 she developed her business "Beyond the Box" which has its own clothing line and production components.

The author has always demonstrated a level of emotional intelligence and empathy beyond her years. She was always passionately persuaded that she could use these attributes to help hurting and misguided young people to heal and develop their confidence and self-worth.

This book represents the culmination of two years of hard work, of commitment to a dream, and an unshakeable conviction that her experiences from adolescence to teenage, could definitely transform and revolutionize the lives of other youth, grappling with the disconcerting challenges of growing pains.

www.ingramcontent.com/pod-product-compliance
Lightning Source LLC
Chambersburg PA
CBHW071912120726
48001CB00005B/1720